RIBBLE MOTOR SERVICES

MIKE RHODES

AMBERLEY

First published 2024

Amberley Publishing
The Hill, Stroud
Gloucestershire, GL5 4EP

www.amberley-books.com

Copyright © Mike Rhodes, 2024

The right of Mike Rhodes to be identified as
the Author of this work has been asserted in
accordance with the Copyrights, Designs and
Patents Act 1988.

ISBN 978 1 3981 2113 3 (print)
ISBN 978 1 3981 2114 0 (ebook)

British Library Cataloguing in Publication Data.
A catalogue record for this book is available from
the British Library.

Typesetting by SJmagic DESIGN SERVICES, India.
Printed in Great Britain.

Introduction

This is not a history of Ribble Motor Services Ltd but a recollection of some of the author's memories and experiences associated with this prestigious operator.

Although I have many early childhood and bus-spotting memories, I did not start taking any meaningful photographic records until 1974. The photographic content therefore spans the years from 1974 to the early 1990s and includes a number of images taken by my good friend and associate of many years Dr Ian Derrick. They are presented in no particular order.

Ribble started from humble beginnings in 1919 from a base in Gregson Lane just 4 miles south of Preston. During the 1920s the company rapidly expanded, mainly with the acquisition of other smaller operators. A garage was opened in Park Road in the centre of Preston in 1921 but this soon became inadequate as the fleet continued to expand. The situation prompted a move to the district of Frenchwood in 1927 where over a period of time a large complex was established which included a running shed capable of holding around 140 vehicles, vehicle mechanical and bodywork repair shops, parts stores, a paint shop, print unit and an imposing administrative building.

Significant gains to the fleet included the takeover of the Waterloo & Crosby Motors Services in 1928 and thus gaining a foothold on Merseyside – being awarded the licence to operate the Carlisle City routes in 1931 and the acquisition of the Blackpool-based concern of W. C. Standerwick in 1932, with the latter remaining a separate subsidiary until 1972. In September 1942 Ribble became part of the British Electric Traction group (BET) and remained as such until the Transport Holding Company was formed in March 1968. Nationalisation then followed on 1 January 1969. Over the years the fleet had expanded to over 1,200 buses and coaches, which were based at thirty garages located across Ribble's vast operating area, which stretched from the border city of Carlisle to Merseyside. Ribble's sphere of operations included stage-carriage, inter-city/town express and long-distance express services supplemented by excursions and extended tours – quite a diverse portfolio.

A later tried and tested company strategy was to establish operating agreements with competing operators rather than any aggressive takeover policies. This was especially significant on Merseyside where the Aintree, Bootle and Liverpool depots provided buses for many of the city's routes alongside the incumbent Liverpool Corporation (later MPTE) buses. Such agreements also existed with some of the local municipal operators such as Accrington (Hyndburn), Barrow, Bolton, Burnley, Fylde Borough, Haslingden, Lancaster, Preston, St Helens and Wigan, along with other such notable operators as Crosville, J. Fishwick & Sons, Lancashire United, North Western and Pennine Motors. Ribble was also an early exponent of 'OMO' with many lightly used, single-deck-operated rural routes being converted to 'One Man (Person) Operation' in the early 1960s.

Not unsurprisingly the Ribble fleet was mainly based on Leyland chassis products. These included Lions, Olympics, Royal Tigers, Tiger Cubs, Leopards and Nationals which formed the backbone of the single-deck fleet for many years. Meanwhile the double-deck fleet included a wide spectrum of Leyland Titans through to the PD3 marque along with their successors, the Atlantean and Olympian. It was only in later NBC years that buses of Bristol manufacture joined the fleet in any significant numbers.

Throughout the 1970s Ribble weathered the storm of nationalisation, but all was not well. The hideous NBC poppy red colour scheme had replaced the Ribble cherry red and cream and the coaches were now painted in an insidious all-over white with 'National Travel' fleetnames. By the 1980s deregulation was looming large. In 1986 the Cumbria operations were transferred to Cumberland Motor Services and likewise the Merseyside operations to the newly formed North Western Road Car Company (1986) – the fleet size had all but been halved at a stroke. This left the company as easy pickings for the emerging private companies and Ribble was snapped up by the rapidly expanding Stagecoach in April 1989. Over thirty years on and it is as if the once mighty Ribble had never existed.

Although the present-day Stagecoach operator still uses the Selborne Street garage, the rest of the Ribble empire has long since vanished into history. As part of the Merseyside and South Lancashire Company group the repainting of buses now generally takes place on Merseyside at the former Liverpool Corporation Gillmoss depot. Other than at Carlisle, Kendal and Morecambe the present-day operator no longer has a garage presence in the region.

As previously mentioned, Ribble had a joint operating agreement with Preston Corporation, which initially involved routes P1 (Frenchwood to Lea), P2 (Fulwood to Penwortham), P4 (Penwortham) and P5 (Hutton to Ribbleton). One Ribble bus was rostered for the P1 service, which was later altered to alternatively serve Lea (later renumbered to P3) and Larches. The P2 was wholly operated by Ribble whilst the P5 was likewise wholly operated by the Corporation. The Penwortham P4 only lasted a few months but the route number was recycled in the mid-1960s for a new route to Ingol, which was operated by a mixture of Ribble and Corporation buses. Additional routes to Ingol (P6) and Savick (P7) were started in the 1970s with Ribble only having a physical involvement in the former. Many a journey was made on the solitary bus that Ribble provided on the P1 which was always allocated to the same duty. The joint service was double-deck operated until converted to 'OMO' on 6 April 1970, from which date all the buses were provided by PCTD.

Having been brought up in the heart of the Ribble domain I have many happy memories of seeing and travelling on Ribble buses. As a small boy in the 1950s a regular journey was made once a fortnight to visit grandparents in Blackburn. The journey would start on a Preston Corporation PD on the jointly operated P1 route, which would take us to the town centre. It would then be a short walk to Tithebarn Street bus station and onwards on a Ribble double-decker on the 150 service. The journey would be repeated in reverse at the end of the day, although the last leg would more often than not be completed on a Corporation PD1 on the Ashton Lane Ends C service.

Tithebarn Street and North Road Express bus stations played host to large numbers of bus arrivals and departures and duplicates on the 'X' series of express routes in the summer months and could produce buses from any garage of Ribble's operating territory. Aintree- and Liverpool-allocated Burlingham-bodied PD3/4s frequently turned up on the X61 whilst buses from the original family of 'White Ladies' (East

Lancs-bodied PD2/3s) were also frequent visitors on services to/from East and North Lancashire and Manchester. The principal service from Manchester was the X60, which ran with many duplicates and also used buses from the fleets of Accrington Corporation (Hyndburn), Lancashire United and North Western Roadcar amongst others. Many of these didn't actually call in at the bus station but could be seen taking the direct avoiding route through Preston along the Arterial (Blackpool) Road (the M55 didn't open until 1975), a journey which could be fraught with traffic hold-ups. The provincial bus stations were closed in October 1969 and all operators' services were transferred to a brand-spanking-new bus station, which featured eighty departure gates (all of the gates were never fully utilised and the west side of the bus station was closed in September 2017 as part of a refurbishment/rationalisation programme).

With the main company workshops situated in Preston, Frenchwood became a natural magnet to catch a glimpse of the latest developments – be it buses from far away garages under repair, newly repainted buses or brand-new buses awaiting acceptance inspections. One of the most lasting memories is of Ribble's first Albion Lowlander, which was parked outside the paint shop in Frenchwood Knoll one Saturday morning in February 1964. In the early 1960s Park Road garage was used as a storage shed for delicensed buses or coaches which were not required for service during the winter months. The garage was usually kept locked and it was the norm to try to peer through the crack between the doors to see what gems lurked inside. However the garage was demolished in the mid-1960s to facilitate the construction of Ring Way and Blackpool's Devonshire Road garage was henceforth used as the main storage base for such vehicles. Withdrawn buses were generally not to be seen at Frenchwood as these were usually stored in the garage yards at Burnley and Morecambe and somewhat later also at Skelmersdale.

Ribble had acquired the operating licence and buses of Scout Motor Services in December 1961 and continued to use their garage premises at Starchhouse Square until 1966/7 (again the site was required for the construction of Ring Way). Many acceptance inspections were carried out of the TCK-registered Metro-Cammell-bodied PD3/5s and Marshall-bodied Leopards in the two-road covered shed throughout 1962–3.

My bus-spotting exploits were not unnaturally confined to the local area in my formative years. However I first ventured further afield in August 1963 armed with a 'Ribble child All-Route-Ticket', which had cost sixteen shillings and was valid for eight days. My adventurous nature took me to Carlisle, Liverpool and Manchester (twice) where I copped some of those elusive Ribble buses which never seemed to venture away from their home territory. Many other trips followed, particularly to Blackpool, which was just an hour away from Ashton Lane Ends on the 155 (via Weeton) or the 158 (via Wrea Green).

In August 1977 I undertook a comprehensive survey of Ribble's bus routes centred on Alston, Ambleside, Carlisle, Grange-over-Sands, Kendal, Penrith, Sedbergh and Ulverston. Again, armed with a weekly ticket, I travelled on and photographed many of the buses which were employed on some of the more obscure routes. These were almost without exception worked by Bristol REs or Leyland Leopards which still dominated the Cumbria region at the time. Some of the pictures taken on this trip have been included in the book. Not long after the ubiquitous Leyland National began to make significant inroads.

Following the creation of the National Bus Company it was really all downhill from then on. As spiralling costs impacted on profitability, along with many other long-established bus companies, Ribble slowly gravitated towards deregulation and revitalisation under a private umbrella. However, long gone was the plethora of company bus liveries with their stylish fleetnames. These had been replaced by insidious poppy red and leaf green (whatever that was) and would now be replaced by even more ill-thought-out colour schemes. Thankfully, although the industry is now dominated by a handful of conglomerate operators, at least some sanity has returned to the modern-day liveries. Firstbus in particular have replicated many a defunct fleet livery on single examples of their Volvo B9TL buses with the reproductions being to an exceedingly high standard. Even Stagecoach entered into the spirit of its Ribble heritage by duly celebrating Ribble's centenary in 2019 and beyond.

There is, however, a very good representation of preserved former Ribble buses dotted around the country and in the North West in particular, with many of the different types which were once so common to be seen in their original colours. One lasting memory for the author was the sight of fifty Ribble buses lined up on the M66 motorway having worked from all parts of Lancashire to Heaton Park for the occasion of Pope John Paul II's Thanksgiving Mass. Oh for a time machine!

Mike Rhodes

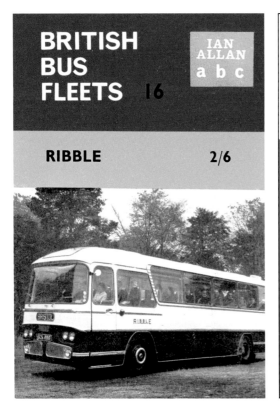

A recreation of a throwback to the early years of Ribble operation. Leyland-bodied Lion CK3825 (No. 295), which was one of a batch of seventy buses purchased in 1927, was photographed in Gregson Lane (not to be confused with the nearby place name which was the original base of Ribble) at Higher Walton as it retraced the course of Ribble's first commercial bus route on 19 September 1982. This was done in conjunction with an open day at the Frenchwood depot complex. Not a car to be seen.

Eastern Coach Works-bodied (ECW) Bristol VRT No. 1445 is seen in Sharoe Green Lane at Preston on 27 March 1992. It was one of a batch of a twenty-three received in 1978/9. This version of the 144 had originated at Blackburn and travelled via Longridge and Goosnargh (having replaced service 11). By the date of this picture Ribble was part of the Stagecoach group.

Ribble was allocated ten of these ECW-bodied Bristol RELH coaches in 1972; they were originally painted in National Travel all-over white. No. 1016, recently transferred from Liverpool to Ulverston, is seen at Newby Bridge on 30 April 1980 with a service for Windermere. Marshall-bodied Leyland Leopard No. 480 has arrived from Grange-over-Sands. (Ian Derrick)

Ribble had many scenic routes throughout the Lake District and none more so than the 649, which ran from Penrith to Patterdale and included sections of route that skirted Ullswater. Kendal-allocated Leopard No. 466 was new in 1963 and is seen climbing away from the lake side in this early 1970s spring rendition. (Ian Derrick)

Ribble received its first batch of Leyland Nationals in 1972 and thereafter many more until the type ceased to be built. No. 729 was new in 1976 and is seen in Eldon Street in Preston on 28 January 1979 having been diverted away from Blackpool Road due to the icy conditions. The erstwhile Empress cinema was closed in the late 1960s and is where the author attended many a Saturday morning film matinee.

The first Leyland Nationals were of a two-door configuration and were allocated to Fleetwood, Preston and Wigan depots. Nos 396 and 400 were photographed on 11 May 1980 in Pharos Street in Fleetwood on local town services. Although Stagecoach maintained a presence in the town into the 2000s, local services were mainly operated by Blackpool Transport Services in 2023.

Burlingham-bodied Leyland PD3/4 No. 1597 was photographed outside the Liverpool Skelhorne Street garage on 23 July 1974 still in Ribble red livery with the last style of cream fleetname. There were 105 of these distinctive-looking workhorses and many of the type were initially allocated to Carlisle and Merseyside garages.

Another proper red Titan, No. 1578 from Aintree garage, is seen on Southport Promenade on the same date. It is working back to Liverpool on service 302, which would take it through Scarisbrick and Maghull. The style of destination screen was somewhat simplistic and specified by Ribble (it resembled a particular piece out of a Meccano set).

Kendal garage supplied the buses for the 517/8 services, which ran from Ambleside/Windermere to Ulverston via Newby Bridge. Veteran Leopard No. 466 is seen in Queen Street close to journey's end on 28 May 1977. Ulverston War Memorial was unveiled in the Market Square on 11 May 1921.

Victoria Road in Ulverston could be a hive of activity with buses departing for various local and not-so-local destinations. On 30 April 1980 two of Ulverston's stable of Leopards are waiting departure. No. 506 is on the jointly operated (with Barrow Borough Transport) service 520 to Barrow whilst No. 521 behind is waiting to depart on the 512 to Coniston. Parked across the road out of service is No. 207. (Ian Derrick)

By the late 1970s Ulverston's Leopard stronghold had been broken with the acquisition of some of the Marshall-bodied Bristol RESLs. No. 323 had previously been allocated to Burnley and is seen in the garage yard at Ulverston with Leopards Nos 527 and 607 on 30 April 1980. Leyland Nationals would also later make an appearance. (Ian Derrick)

Some of Merseyside Ribble's journeys terminated at St John's Lane whilst others continued down to Pier Head. ECW-bodied Atlantean No. 1503 was delivered new to Merseyside in 1981. It is seen at Mann Island on 21 September 1985 with a service for Netherton.

In January 1969 Carlisle garage acquired the routes and buses of the city's United Automobile outstation. This added twenty-one buses of Bristol RE and LS types to the garage strength. Bristol RE No. 279, now in full Ribble livery, was originally United Auto No. BU696 and is seen working a Carlisle city local route from Garlands Hospital. These buses had all been withdrawn by 1975. (Ian Derrick)

A general view of buses parked up at Carlisle's Lowther Street bus station. All but the last of the 1971/2 ECW-bodied Bristol VRTs were delivered painted in Ribble livery, as shown on No. 1992. Former United Bristol RE No. 277 has been repainted into NBC corporate colours, as has Willowbrook-bodied Leopard DP No. 910. (Ian Derrick)

The 555 from Kendal to Keswick was one of Ribble's flagship routes and was operated by buses from Ambleside, Kendal and Lancaster garages. The buses employed in the late 1970s were generally a mixture of Atlanteans of varying ages and body styles. On 21 April 1976 the passengers onboard were treated to a ride on Kendal's 1962 Metro-Cammell-bodied lowbridge Atlantean No. 1807, which is seen in Rydal Road in Ambleside.

No. 1807 is seen again in this line-up, which was photographed inside Blackburn's George Street garage. Also on view is No. 1811 of the same batch and Bristol VRTs Nos 1983/92. The three former Carlisle deckers had been ousted by a new intake of Atlanteans and Bristol VRTs in 1978–80. (Ian Derrick)

Ribble's last Leopard saloons were thirty dual-purpose versions which were bodied by the Loughborough firm of Willowbrook in 1967/8. No. 907 was latterly allocated to Ulverston for a number of years and was photographed working a local route on the town's Mountbarrow estate on 30 April 1980. (Ian Derrick)

Two years later and No. 907 had been sold out of service. It is now owned by the Crusaders Bible Group and is seen on display behind Ribble's Frenchwood paint shop on 20 June 1982.

Ribble's last batch of saloon Leopards consisted of Nos 628–82 and were of a shorter configuration fitted with forty-four-seat bodies constructed by Marshalls; they were generally employed on rural routes. No. 652 was photographed in Percy Street in Preston on 5 March 1978 and had worked over from Clitheroe on service 9, which would have taken it through Longridge and Grimsargh.

A considerable number of the short Leopards were based at the Lake District garages. In the 1970s Ambleside garage had six of the type to work its rural routes. No. 658 is seen departing Coniston on 20 June 1976 on the 505, which was routed via Hawkshead.

Ribble received a batch of twenty Burlingham-bodied Leyland PS2s in 1950. They were retired from service in the early 1960s. Whilst three passed to Southport Corporation and were converted to open-top buses, three more were converted by Ribble to breakdown tenders. No. BD1 had been No. 2778 (renumbered to 228) and commenced its new role in December 1964. In this view it has been sent to rescue Titan No. 1735, which had expired outside St Peter's Church in Fylde Road in Preston on 30 August 1974.

Service 167 operated from Preston to Blackpool (previously Lytham) via Freckleton, Lytham and St Annes. ECW-bodied Olympian No. 2134, which was new in 1983, is seen in Park Street (Lytham Square) at Lytham on 12 July 1983 on its way back to Preston. This scene was virtually unchanged in 2023.

No. 607 was the last of the 1965 Weymann-bodied Leopards. Having been transferred from Preston, it is seen on local route 524 in Biglands Drive on the Croftlands estate in Ulverston on 11 August 1977 having worked the 17.40 from Victoria Road.

Ribble/Standerwick's fleet of 'Gay Hostess' Weymann-bodied Atlanteans took to the road in 1960 to take advantage of the faster new stretches of motorway. They were retired in 1971/2 and around a dozen were snapped up by Teesside (Cleveland Transit). Former Standerwick No. 36 (Teesside No. H65) was photographed in Stockton-on-Tees High Street on 20 May 1978. Ribble's simple destination display has been replaced by a more detailed arrangement and only a small part of the original skirt mouldings remain.

Lancaster's Leopards wandered far and wide and could be seen as far north as Keswick, as far south as Preston and as far east as Skipton on a regular basis. No. 216 was crossing the WCML in Carnforth when it was photographed on service 550 to nearby Warton, just 1.5 miles further on, on 18 July 1978.

No. 216 again, this time it is seen in Tabley Lane approaching the village of Woodplumpton near Preston on 9 April 1980. It is working the 16.40 182 service from Preston to Great Eccleston via Woodplumpton, Catforth and Elswick, which was a filling in turn for Lancaster garage.

The Albion Lowlander was not the most aesthetic-looking bus and Ribble had sixteen (not counting the former demonstrator acquired from BBMS) of the type join the fleet in two batches in 1964–5. Wigan garage had a strong association with the type in the early 1970s. No. 1859 is seen in Carlisle Street in Preston on 9 July 1977 displaying a school service number.

Similar bus No. 1853 was recorded in Lytham Road in Fulwood on 26 August 1976 on the jointly operated (with Borough of Preston) P6 service to Ingol Redcar Avenue. There were only three journeys each way on Monday to Friday on this service. Ribble operated the 15.20 and 18.00 departures to Ingol and the 18.25 back from Ingol. The Albion is seen on the early evening journey.

The dual-door Bristol RELL was another type which was somewhat alien to Ribble. Nevertheless the soon-to-be nationalised company received no fewer than forty of the type in 1968–69. They were used on 'OPO' services in Bootle, Carlisle, Chorley, Fleetwood, Ormskirk and Preston. No. 223 is seen outside Fleetwood garage on 20 March 1977.

Bootle's small allocation of the type was used mainly on local routes to the area, although they did make incursions into the city centre, particularly on the 57A from Netherton. No. 239 was photographed in Linacre Lane in Bootle on circular service 48 on 17 July 1978. The last of the type were not withdrawn until *c.* 1982.

Ribble received a further forty ECW-bodied Bristol RESLs in 1971–72; these were single-door models and were distributed throughout the operating area. No. 336 is seen in the erstwhile Blackburn Boulevard bus station on 22 April 1982 on service 244, which ran from Rochdale to Preston.

The later Bristols were the last buses to be received in Ribble red as repainting into NBC colours began in earnest in 1972. No. 351 was the only one of the type allocated to Lancaster at the time and was photographed in the city's Damside bus station on 10 August 1974. The full length of service 580 ran from Morecambe to Skipton via Ingleton and Settle and was jointly operated with Pennine Motors of Gargrave.

Lowheight Atlantean PDR1s Nos 1801–14 were bodied by Metro-Cammell and joined the fleet in 1962. Kendal's No. 1807 is seen again on the 555 at the south end of the route departing Lancaster on 21 August 1976. Just short of three hours was allowed in the schedule for the 45-mile journey to Keswick.

Prior to receiving three of the Northern Counties-bodied Atlanteans, Penrith's double-deck allocation consisted of lowbridge buses Nos 1663, 1805/6. No. 1805 was photographed on the north bank of Ullswater in September 1977 working a 649 journey from Penrith to Patterdale, a journey of some fifty minutes. Ullswater is the second largest lake in the Lake District. (Ian Derrick)

Some of Ribble's rural routes were quite obscure. Short Leopard No. 670 is seen on 9 August 1977 on a short layover in the village of Morland, which is some 8 miles south-east of Penrith. This service, which ran to nearby Newby, consisted of just two return journeys on Tuesdays only.

One of Ambleside's sextet of short Leopards, No. 680, is seen climbing out of the town on service 516 to Dungeon Ghyll. This popular service was still running in 2023 and was operated by Stagecoach. This view was unchanged nearly fifty years later. (Ian Derrick)

Following a brief flirtation with the Albion Lowlander, Ribble then bought two small batches of Atlantean PDR1/2s consisting of ten with Alexander 'H' bodies in 1966 and fifteen with Northern Counties bodies in 1967. One of the latter, No. 1961, was photographed at Milnthorpe on 30 April 1980.

At one time Penrith garage had three of the type on its books and they were often employed on the 615 to Carlisle or the 649 to Patterdale or, as seen here, on the local town service 646. No. 1954 is seen in Castle Hill Road on 13 August 1977 working its way round the 646 circular route. At the time Nos 1961/3 were also allocated to Penrith.

Ribble introduced its famous long-distance motorway services to London in April 1960 with a fleet of 'Gay Hostess' Atlanteans. Some of the buses carried Scout and Standerwick fleetnames. These were phased out in 1971/2 and replaced by thirty not-so-reliable Bristol VRL double-deck coaches. Now painted in National white, No. 76 is seen alongside Plaxton-bodied Leopard coach No. 81 at Devonshire Road in Blackpool on 8 January 1977. A number of coaches were usually delicensed in the winter months.

In 1974 seven of the type were based at Burnley garage with the other twenty-three operating out of Blackpool Devonshire Road. Service numbers were not displayed on the buses but the route network served most of the principal towns in Lancashire. No. 73 is seen in Finchley Road at West Hampstead in London on 6 June 1977 making its way towards Victoria coach station. Nos 62–4 passed to the Tyne & Wear PTE, who used them on a service to the Tyne Quay.

At one point Ribble standardised on Leyland's PD2/3 model and bought fifty lowbridge buses in 1950/1. They were fifty-three seaters with platform doors and gave around fifteen years of service, eventually being replaced by the Leopards. No. 1349 was saved for preservation and is seen in Birley Street in Preston on 14 July 1978 before embarking on an overnight trip to London via the A6 as support vehicle for a sponsored cycle ride to the capital. (Ian Derrick)

Ribble's coach purchases included a batch of thirty-five Harrington Cavalier-bodied Leopards in 1961. The first twenty had thirty-two seats whilst the remainder had forty-one. First of the intake was No. 1019, which passed to PMT (Potteries Motor Traction) in 1972. Then bearing the number 23, it was photographed resting in the Stoke-on-Trent PMT garage on 29 March 1975 – still basically in Ribble livery.

When deregulation arrived in October 1986 Ribble was already ahead of the game. In a short period of time the operator added sixty-four minibuses to its fleet. These were built by Mercedes-Benz with Reeve Burgess nineteen- or twenty-seat bodies. New groups of routes under the 'Mini-Link' banner were introduced in several towns. No. 529 was one of thirteen of the type allocated to Kendal for services in Kendal and Windermere. It was photographed in Blackhall Road in Kendal on 30 June 1987.

Another twelve of the type were allocated to Fleetwood garage for a new network of local services based on Cleveleys, Thornton and Fleetwood. No. 541 demonstrates the attractive livery in Queen's Terrace at Fleetwood on 25 July 1987.

Preston's Ingol estate was built in the early 1960s and was first served by a bus route on 13 February 1965. Numbered P4, the route was jointly operated with Preston Corporation. It initially ran to an infrequent timetable and only as far as Barry Avenue. It was extended to Dunbar Drive from 25 June 1966. No. 1973 (S5) was one of five MCCW-bodied Atlanteans acquired from Scout Motors in 1968. It is seen in Creswell Avenue on the estate on 5 March 1976. In 2023 it was part of the RVPT collection.

Bristol RESL No. 322 was based at Blackburn in 1979 having previously been at Chorley. It was photographed on 30 June on the B6243 near Spade Mill Reservoir(s) having not long left Longridge. Service 11 was a somewhat circuitous route between Preston and Blackburn which took in the delights of Goosnargh, Longridge, Ribchester and Wilpshire.

In 1951 Ribble took delivery of its largest ever single vehicle order comprising 120 Leyland-bodied Royal Tiger coaches with centre entrances. No. 899 was the penultimate bus and entered service in December and was withdrawn in November 1962. After a spell working for A & C McClennan of Spitalfield it was saved for preservation and brought south of the border. It is pictured in a field at Catterall on 1 October 1975.

Another twenty-three VRTs arrived in 1978/9, which were in the main allocated to Carlisle and Morecambe garages. Nos 1441/3 from Morecambe are seen outside the Butler Street 1850 East Lancashire Railway station entrance at Preston (long since demolished) on 11 April 1982 whilst employed on rail replacement duties.

There is the sum total of just six people (and a dog) in this picture, which would indicate it was recorded early on a Sunday morning (note the clock). In the background the stalls of Preston's annual pot fair can just be discerned. Park Royal-bodied Atlantean No. 1393 is seen heading down the bus lane in upper Friargate on 26 August 1984. The Harris Library & Museum in the background was designed by James Hibbert and completed in 1893.

Still working in Carlisle in 1979 was lowbridge Atlantean No. 1809, which was photographed turning out of Warwick Road into The Crescent on 4 April. It is working city service 661 from Morton West to Harraby East.

Ribble's Burlingham-bodied Leyland PD3/4s were a popular choice with operators who scoured the second-hand market. Even China Motor Bus in Hong Kong obtained six of the type third hand for use mainly as Driver Tuition Vehicles. London Country, however, managed to assemble no fewer than twenty of the type for the same purpose. *Above:* LR14 had been No. 1588 in the Ribble fleet and was acquired by LCBS in July 1976. It is seen passing Southed-on-Sea bus station on 9 June 1977. It was sold to Wombwell Diesels for scrap in May 1980. *Below:* The former No. 1571 became LR18 in the LCBS fleet. It was used from September 1976 until July 1979 when it too was sold to Wombwell Diesels, which is where it was photographed on 10 September 1979.

ECW-bodied Bristol VRL No. 58 was on a private charter working when photographed at Ashton Lane Ends in Preston on 1 April 1976. At this time the whole fleet carried Standerwick fleetnames even though the operator had been fully absorbed back in December 1972.

The National VRLs occasionally turned up at Frenchwood. No. 69 was photographed at Selborne Street on 23 August 1976. These buses had forty-two seats on the upper deck and just eighteen arranged around a number of tables on the lower deck. No. 60 has survived into preservation. Even on these buses the destination screens were minimal.

On 20 June 1982 Ribble held an open day at its Frenchwood complex. These two pictures show Leyland Nationals receiving attention in what originally was the paint shop and was then being utilised for engineering work. *Above:* No. 407 was one of the original batch of dual-door Nationals received in 1972/3; it was being fitted with an experimental access ramp. *Below:* No. 887 was the latest new National to join the fleet and was undergoing an acceptance inspection. The paint shop had been opened in 1962 and was capable of holding around ten buses at a time as they passed through the various stages of repainting. The complex was closed in 1989 and subsequently demolished.

Deregulation brought more services and an influx of second-hand double-deckers to work them. These were a mixture of Bristol VRTs, Daimler CRGs and Atlanteans. The latter were obtained from a variety of sources including Southdown. Looking very much like Ribble's original Park Royal-bodied machines, No. 1602, which had been No. 702 in the Southdown fleet, was parked at the back of Preston bus station on 30 December 1988.

The takeover by Stagecoach in April 1989 did nothing to stem the tide of imported second-hand Atlanteans. A large contingent of former G M Buses' Atlanteans was pressed into service in this uncharacteristic green livery, having been obtained at least third hand. Again seen at Preston bus station, No. 1678 had started life as GMPTE No. 7603. It was later converted to an open-top bus and operated for The Big Bus Company in London.

The 'TCK' PD3/5s were new in 1963 and had seventy-two-seat MCCW bodies. They later acquired the name of 'Tanks' due to their robust construction. In 1978 No. 1821 was one of Morecambe's small stable of PD3/5s and was seen in Regent Road in the town centre on service 570 from Heysham to Lancaster.

No. 1758 was one of the 1962 batch of PD3/5s and was allocated to Bootle garage in the mid-1970s. It was photographed in Ormskirk Road at Aintree on a service 321 journey from Lydiate to Walton Church from where it would presumably proceed empty to Bootle garage.

A snowy scene in Preston on 14 December 1981 as ECW-bodied Bristol VRT No. 2027 is seen gingerly making slow progress up Fishergate Hill. Service 108 was a recently introduced route following a reorganisation of services to Hutton, Longton and Penwortham.

Another VRT from the same batch, No. 2022, was photographed outside Blackpool's Devonshire Road garage on 5 June 1982. This was one of a number of buses from different Lancashire bus fleets that were used to promote the 'Red Rose Rambler' ticket, which could also be used on local trains. Devonshire Road garage was closed just five years later and the site has since been redeveloped.

Leyland National No. 821 was one of a batch of ten forty-four-seaters received in 1980. It is seen in Blackburn Boulevard on 16 July 1980. Service 215 to Bolton ran via Darwen and Astley Bridge. Bristol RESL No. 317 can be seen behind on the service 11 stand to Preston.

Preston was one of the first three garages to receive an allocation of Leyland Nationals. No. 439 was new in 1973 and is seen at Ashton Lane Ends on the jointly operated P4 service from Ingol on 2 November 1980. This was the last day Ribble vehicles worked on the route and the following day it operated as service 34 (44 in the evening and on Sundays).

A batch of twenty Weymann-bodied Leyland PDR1/1 Atlanteans arrived in 1962. These were in a reverse livery of the normal red and cream and were again known as 'White Ladies'. They were based at garages which provided buses for express routes such as the X14, X30, X40, X43, X50, X60 and X61. In the early 1970s they were demoted to ordinary stage-carriage work and No. 1272 was caught on camera in Blackpool Road in Preston on 5 July 1977 working on service 154 to Blackpool.

Similar bus No. 1284 was captured on film at Preston bus station on 7 August 1976 displaying information for the 145 to Whittingham. Ribble's 'Meccano' style destination screens were just about as basic as they could be with just enough room for the ultimate destination. These buses retained their coach seats until withdrawal in the late 1970s.

One of the early Bristol VRTs, which was first allocated to Carlisle when new in 1971, is seen at the bottom of Fishergate Hill in Preston on 26 March 1982. No. 1980 was transferred south to Preston in 1978 and service 104 had previously been the P20 (P2) jointly operated route to Penwortham.

Similar vehicle No. 1988 is seen at Ashton Lane Ends on 1 November 1980 on the P4 service from Ingol. This was just two days before Ribble buses ceased to be used on the route. Over its long period of involvement with the route (fifteen years) Ribble had turned out a bewildering selection of buses, particularly on a Sunday, which had even included a rare appearance of a Gay Hostess Atlantean and several coach types.

In 1954 Ribble bought fifteen Burlingham Seagull-bodied Tiger Cub coaches. These were followed by a further twenty-six in 1956 and another thirty-two in 1958. No. 975 belonged to the 1956 batch and was fitted with forty-one seats. It was withdrawn in February 1968 and eventually passed into preservation. It was photographed in Cable Street in the centre of Lancaster on 21 June 1981.

The latter batch was numbered 987 to 1018. The former No. 1009 was sold out of service in May 1969 and had latterly been used by Wimpey as a staff bus. It was later purchased by dealer F. Cowley and is seen in his yard at Heywood on 11 September 1974. On the left is a former Southdown 1959 Harrington Crusader-bodied Commer Avenger, which was disposed of by Southdown in 1971.

Another of the first batch of Albions, No. 1852, is seen at the back of Preston bus station on 29 June 1976. This twelve-year-old bus was still looking very smart but would only have another two years left in service.

Pride of place in the Ribble Vehicle Preservation Trust's (RVPT) preserved vehicle running fleet must surely go to this pre-war Leyland TD5. No. 2057 was another fifty-three-seat lowbridge bus which was bodied by Burlingham in 1939 (rebodied by Alexander in 1949). It was withdrawn from service in August 1960. It is seen in St Annes on 28 August 2017 on a vintage running day service from Lytham Hall.

Ribble buses and signposts. *Above:* MCCW-bodied Leyland PD3/5 No. 1784 takes a breather outside the Boar's Head at Hoghton on 5 July 1979 on its journey from Preston to Blackburn. The sign is pointing to Samlesbury and Hoghton Bottoms. The original sign pole still exists, although the fingerposts have been changed. *Below:* Many miles away in Cumbria Marshall-bodied Leyland Leopard No. 682 of Ambleside garage was photographed on the B5286 at Pullwood Bay passing another sign giving directions to Ambleside, Coniston, Hawkshead and Tarn Hows. Although a sign still exists at this location, it is not the one shown in the picture. Service 505 still ran between Coniston and Ambleside/Windermere/Kendal in 2023 seven days a week and was operated by Stagecoach. (Ian Derrick)

On 2 July 1979 a lightning strike brought all services at Preston to a halt. Parked (abandoned) on the bus station forecourt were Leopard No. 494, Titan No. 1766, National No. 439 and Bristol RE No. 328.

Uniformity is well and truly demonstrated in this picture recorded on 1 October 1977. Seen from one of the car park upper levels at Preston bus station are Leyland Nationals Nos 428, 435, 771, 398, 740, 700, 699 and 448. The Park Royal-bodied Atlantean is No. 1322. The brick building behind the buses was John Booth's foundry (the building was owned by Dorman Smith), which was eventually demolished in 1980. A new retail store was built on the site which has since had a number of owners including Tradex, Sainsbury's and B&M Bargains.

In November 1980 Ribble received two thirty-five-seat ECW-bodied Bristol LHSs, numbered 271/2, for specific use on routes based in Clitheroe. One of the local routes was referred to as 'Betty's Bus', which was named after one of the regular drivers. No. 272 is seen at Frenchwood on 20 June 1982. Following bus deregulation in October 1986 No. 271 was transferred to Ulverston whilst No. 272 moved to Kendal.

Following hot on the heels of the sixty-four Mercedes minibuses was a further order for forty Freight Rover Sherpas with diminutive sixteen-seat Dormobile bodies. These were again used to supplement the many Mini-Link schemes which were introduced after deregulation. They had very short operating lives with Ribble. No. 574 was photographed in Preston bus station on 19 June 1987.

The original Frenchwood running shed in Selborne Street was built in 1927. It was extended in 1929 and again in 1953. On 2 October 1977 former Bamber Bridge Motor Services' lowbridge Atlantean No. 1967 and Leyland PD3/5 No. 1768 awaited their next turns of duty. The shed was much the same in 2023 and was in use by Ribble's successor, Stagecoach.

In 1966 Ribble bought a batch of ten Leyland PDR1/2 Atlanteans with the somewhat unusual choice of Alexander's 'H' style of bodywork. The ten buses were dotted about Ribble's operating area. No. 1869 is seen in Victoria Street in Preston on a school working to Blessed John Southworth Secondary School on 11 October 1977. No. 1869 had previously been allocated to Lancaster whilst Nos 1870/1/4–6 were frequent performers on the 555 service from Ambleside and Kendal garages.

Besides the five Atlanteans which Ribble acquired from Scout in 1968 they also acquired five Burlingham-bodied PD3s. These remained in service until 1975. The former No. 1978 (S25) was operating for Lloyds of Bagillt when photographed on 1 September 1977. Former Blackpool Transport PD2 No. 311 is alongside. It went for scrap in June 1981.

Clitheroe garage had a small contingent of Leopards and these would frequently be turned out on service 9 from Clitheroe to Preston. No. 597 was one of the 1965 batch which was bodied by Weymann. It is seen at Knowle Green, between Longridge and Hurst Green, on 30 June 1979.

As previously mentioned Bristol VRTs Nos 1979–2001 were delivered new to Carlisle in 1971/2 to accelerate the conversion of Carlisle's city routes to 'OPO'. Whilst Nos 1979–2000 were the last deckers delivered new in Ribble red, No. 2001 was the first to appear in poppy red, in July 1972. They were replaced by new Atlanteans and Bristol VRTs in 1978/9 with the majority ending up at Blackburn, Clitheroe and Preston. No. 1993 was first photographed in West Tower Street in Carlisle on 8 August 1977 (*above*) and then again in Lancaster Road in Preston on 31 August 1979 (*below*). The P20 had come into being on 14 August 1978 with the renumbering of the jointly operated P2 service.

The whole of the batch of PD3/5s Nos 1756–1800 were fitted with illuminated side advertisement panels whilst the later batch Nos 1815–50 weren't. No. 1787 has a blank panel and is seen in St John's Lane in the centre of Liverpool on 17 July 1978.

A bit of a tight squeeze for Leyland Titan No. 1739 as it sets off back from Chipping on service 10 to Preston on 30 June 1979. In 2023 there was no direct bus service from Chipping to Preston and a change of bus and operator had to be made at Longridge to complete the same journey.

No. 727 was one of a batch of twenty-two Harrington-bodied Leopard coaches purchased in 1963. They were replaced by a similar number of Duple-bodied Leopards in 1974. This particular bus passed to O. K. Motors Services of Bishop Auckland and had brought a coach load of day-trippers to Blackpool on 7 October 1978.

No. 731 had been part of a large batch of Plaxton-bodied Leopards which joined the fleet in 1963/4. This particular bus had originally been allocated to the Standerwick fleet but was later transferred to the Ribble fleet in February 1968. Seen painted in the colours of Ingleby's of York, No. 731 is seen at Leeds on 13 September 1981 from where it participated in a road run to York. Founded in 1968, Ingleby's Luxury Coaches was still trading in 2023.

Service 761 was a mimic of the old X61, which back in the day had run between Liverpool and Blackpool via Ormskirk, Preston, Lytham and St Annes. Leyland Olympians Nos 2156–9 were painted in this attractive 'Timesaver' livery and virtually brand-new No. 2158 was caught in Friargate in Preston on 25 August 1984. Nos 2157–9 were later moved to Burnley for the 743 and were replaced by some of the red 'Timesaver' buses whilst No. 2156 was based at Kendal.

Another ten 'Timesaver' Olympians arrived in 1985 but these were finished in a red version of the colour scheme. Amongst the routes regularly operated were the 555 (Kendal-based buses) and 761 (Preston-based). However No. 2177 was photographed alongside Ullswater with No. 2175 also in view on the left on a private hire working. No. 2156 and a Tiger coach were also part of the hire group. (Ian Derrick)

Cunningham Bus Services of Paisley acquired at least four examples of the Burlingham-bodied PD3/4s in the mid-1970s. What had been No. 1541 in the Ribble fleet was given the number 66 by Cunningham when it joined the operator in January 1976. The Titan was photographed in Hurst Street in Renfrew on 23 April 1976. It was bound for Renfrew Ferry.

Southend Transport hired three former Ribble Burlinghams from Ensignbus, the former Nos 1533/59/76. The destination screen layout was altered accordingly. No. 317 (1533) is seen in Southend bus station on 1 February 1975. After service in Southend they were exported to Hong Kong, along with No. 1582, and used by China Motorbus as training vehicles.

The original Bootle garage was gained with the acquisition of the Merseyside Touring Company in 1930. However the depot had outgrown its usefulness over the years and was replaced by a brand-new facility in 1979, which had been built just 300 yards further along Hawthorne Road. Leyland National No. 876 is seen in the garage yard on 1 April 1984.

Leyland Nationals Nos 854–77 were new in 1981/2 and were fitted with forty-four seats. Still going strong in the Stagecoach fleet in 1994 was No. 866, which was painted in this '75 years' commemorative livery and was photographed departing Preston bus station with a service bound for Chorley on 26 April.

Ribble received its first Olympian in 1980 with delivery of a further seventy-nine following between 1981 and 1985. The year 1983 produced a small batch of seven comprising Nos 2131–7. The majority of the Olympians were seventy-seven seaters. No. 2132 is seen in Queen's Terrace in Fleetwood on 14 July 1985, bound for Blackpool.

Similar bus No. 2107 was heading out to Penwortham on 19 February 1983 when it caught the photographer's eye at the bottom of Fishergate Hill in Preston. This one was new in 1981. No. 2101 is now preserved and is an active member of the RVPT's collection of restored buses.

The NBC poppy red and white was somewhat lost on the dual-purpose Leopards which had richly suited their previous Ribble red and cream livery. On 14 July 1980 No. 911 was photographed in Fell Lane in Penrith having worked in from the village of Cliburn.

Seen just a few months later, on 5 October, in Burnley garage yard are Nos 906 and 929. Nos 904–33 were bodied by Willowbrook in 1967/8 and were the last Leopards to join the Ribble fleet. Both buses were on home turf and would appear to have been last used on two of the jointly operated (with Burnley & Pendle) routes.

Over the extended weekend of 28–30 April 1984 the railway line between Preston and Blackpool was closed to facilitate the renewal of the Waterloo Road 'Danger' bridge. A rail replacement bus service was jointly provided by Preston Bus and Ribble. ECW-bodied Atlantean No. 1418 is depicted in Butler Street on 28 April. The picture predates the construction of Fishergate Shopping Centre.

A later addition to the Ribble fleet was Atlantean No. 1475, which was one of a batch of new buses drafted into Carlisle in 1979 to work the local city services. It is seen at the Harraby terminus of service 662 in Mallyclose Drive on a snowy 9 January 1982.

Above: By 1974 Kendal had received five of the Marshall-bodied Bristol RESLs in lieu of Leopards. These were Nos 291/4/5/7 and 329. The first of the group, No. 291, is seen in the tiny hamlet of Crosthwaite on 10 August 1977 having worked the 13.15 WF0 from Kendal. This location is now somewhat unrecognisable with the phone box and telegraph poles having been removed and the adjacent barn rebuilt as living accommodation.

Right: The other three Lake District garages – Ambleside, Penrith and Ulverston – also received a smattering of Bristols. No. 323 was transferred from Burnley to Ulverston whilst No. 303 came from Preston. They could appear on any of the services which radiated out of Ulverston. This one is a bit of a mystery as the 512 was not routed via Pullwood Bay, which is where this picture of No. 323 was recorded. It may have travelled from Ulverston to Ambleside as a 517/8 and was now working back as a 505 to Coniston where it might have changed to a 512 for the onward journey back to Ulverston. (Ian Derrick)

Leyland National No. 733 was photographed at Blackburn Boulevard whilst working a journey on the 150 from Preston to Burnley on 22 April 1982. The distinctive concrete bus shelters were demolished in 1996 and several years later a new bus station was opened in nearby Salford (street name).

Many of Ribble's redundant Leopards passed to Passenger Vehicle Sales (PVS) of Barnsley for resale. Camms Coaches of Nottingham acquired a number of former Ribble Leopards. No. 496 is seen parked in a Nottingham side street near the depot on 10 November 1979, not exactly looking pristine.

The majority of the 1955/6 MCCW-bodied Leyland PD2/13s were replaced by new Bristol RESLs in 1970/1. However Nos 1385/91/2/9 were retired from active service in August 1970 and were first used as mobile classrooms in connection with the impending decimalisation of the UK's currency. They later took up duties as Driver Training Vehicles. The former No. 1391 (TU4) was photographed in Carlisle bus station on 4 April 1979. Nos 1381–405/26–30 had been fitted with platform doors from new.

Similar bus No. 1392 (TU1/TD5) was still in use by Ribble as late as 1985 and is seen in Preston bus station on 5 October. Over a period of time Ribble's training fleet had also consisted of a number of Leopards and Burlingham-bodied PD3s.

Plaxton-bodied Leopard coach No. 874 was photographed outside Grange-over-Sands railway station on 28 May 1977. It is either waiting for a private party or has just dropped one off. It was allocated to Penrith garage at the time.

Duple-bodied Leopard No. 1027 was new to Ribble in 1973. In this view it is taking a rest in Albert Road alongside Grange Ribble garage. The X99 ran between Barrow and Manchester (previously Lancaster), which is where No. 1027 was based. The garage was acquired in 1958 with the coaching arm of the Grange Motor & Cycle Company and survived until around 1994. (Ian Derrick)

Continuing the theme of Ribble's exiled Burlinghams, No. 1532 passed to Granby Garments of Wrexham for use as staff transport. Granby's had started up in 1953 making clothes for M&S. It is seen near Wrexham General railway station on 2 September 1981.

Another of Cunningham's quartet of ex-Ribble Burlingham's, No. 1542 (61), was photographed in the centre of Paisley on 10 May 1975 having been purchased in July 1974. Cunningham's operated local bus services in the area from the 1920s until 1979 when the operator was purchased by Western SMT.

Having purchased a single Iveco Daily in 1986 (No. 565), Ribble then purchased another twenty in 1987, which were fitted with Carlyle bodies, ten with twenty-one and ten with twenty-five seats, and painted in a new livery of yellow and red. No. 629 was the last of the second batch and is seen alongside the TSS Manxman on Preston Dock on 16 August 1987.

Next followed a batch of fourteen Dormobile-bodied Dodge/Renaults, again in 1987. Only two other new minibuses joined the Ribble fleet after these but Ribble did acquire a vast number of second-hand Minis from Bee Line and Zippy in 1988. The Preston Port Way Park & Ride commenced running in January 1989 and was operated by Ribble/Stagecoach until it passed to Preston Bus on 28 January 1991. No. 643 is seen outside the Public Hall in Lune Street on 11 February 1989, the original starting point for the service.

Leyland National No. 800 was an ex-demonstrator that was acquired by Ribble in February 1979. Produced as a test bed for the Mark 2, it was a long-time resident of Burnley garage, which is where it is seen on 10 March 1979 when new. After a long operating career with Ribble/ Stagecoach it later passed to North Bank Travel of Hull. (Ian Derrick)

Also seen at Burnley on the same day is Hants & Dorset No. 3085. This had been No. 796 in the Ribble fleet and was a Plaxton-bodied Leopard coach which had been new in 1965. It was transferred from the Standerwick fleet in February 1972 having carried the number 66 and before that 796S. (Ian Derrick)

A comparison in liveries on Burlingham-bodied PD3/4s Nos 1588 and 1597, which were photographed at Skelhorne Street garage in Liverpool on 23 July 1974. No. 1588 was repainted in NBC colours in May 1973 and passed to LCBS in January 1976 and joined the training fleet as LR14 (see page 32). No. 1597 retained its Ribble identity until the end.

Preston's group of MCCW-bodied PD3/5s could be seen in everyday service on a variety of routes right up until the final day in September 1981. No. 1848 (ex-Aintree) has just dropped off a lady passenger in Clifton Village on 9 April 1980 whilst working the Blackpool service via Weeton.

A handful of first-generation Atlanteans lingered on in service into the late 1970s/early 1980s. No. 1686 had been new in 1960 and was still being used on front-line services in 1979. On 26 June it was about to pull away from the stop on Ring Way in Preston whilst working a service 102 journey to Southport. The 102 only had a minor deviation from the similar service 100. Stagecoach provided the same service with its route 2 in 2023.

Ribble didn't really adhere to the trend of advertising liveries, with only a handful of buses being so adorned in the 1970s. Bucking the trend was the last numbered of the 1960 Atlanteans, No. 1700. It was photographed in Garstang Road in Preston on 19 July 1974, close to its final destination. It was withdrawn in 1977 and passed to a dealer.

Preston Bus withdrew the Broadgate service on Sundays and in the evenings from 13 June 1983 and Ribble's 104/8 services to Penwortham were diverted at these times to fill the gap. National No. 460 was about to turn round at the end of Broadgate when photographed on 17 July 1983. This was the last of the 1973/4 batch of forty Nationals.

The service to Ingol Redcar Avenue was the last service to remain jointly operated with Borough of Preston. Leyland National No. 738 was working the 15.20 departure from town when photographed at the junction of Cadley Causeway and Woodplumpton Road on 7 May 1984. It remained jointly operated until the implementation of deregulation on 26 October 1986.

Wardline or Ward Bros was a small independent coach operator based at Lepton near Huddersfield. They also ran a haulage business. In 1962 Ribble bought a small batch of six Leopard coaches with Duple Northern bodies numbered 701–6. The former Nos 702/6 are seen at Ward's garage on 27 February 1976. The former had in the past been allocated by Ribble as the regular Preston North End team bus.

Local Preston service the P2 from Fulwood to Penwortham was in the hands of Atlantean No. 1640 on 8 July 1977. It has just left the Fulwood turning circle in Lightfoot Lane and is about to cross over the WCML railway bridge. The turning circle was first used in May 1977 but passengers were not carried between the last two stops until November. The route was transferred to operation by Borough of Preston from 17 April 1978.

The 555 service has already been featured in this book. Here we see Ambleside's Leopard No. 617 (which had previously been a Preston-based bus) at the stone shelter in the centre of Grasmere with the 14.10 departure. Only another two hours and twenty minutes before it would have reached its final destination when it would have to travel back north again, arriving back at Ambleside at 19.18. (Ian Derrick)

Another view in the heart of the Lake District. Ambleside's short Leopard No. 658 is seen passing the entrance to the Pullwood Bay Estate on a service 505 journey from Ambleside to Coniston. Established in 1891, the estate was the home of Sir William Crossley who, along with his brother Francis, set up the firm of Crossley Brothers in 1867, which later became Crossley Motors.

Service 519 was possibly Ribble's shortest route and for most of the day just ran between Windermere station and Bowness Pier, a journey of just eleven minutes in each direction. Ambleside's Short Leopard No. 680 was still in Ribble red when photographed at Bowness Pier in 1973. Certain journeys went to/from Ambleside to swap vehicles/drivers. (Ian Derrick)

There were four Burlinghams still working out of Preston garage in 1974: Nos 1594/602/4/5. The former was the only one of the quartet which was not painted in NBC colours. No. 1602 was the last in use at Preston and was withdrawn in 1976. No. 1594 is seen alongside the soon-to-be-completed Crest Hotel in Tithebarn Street. (Ian Derrick)

Ribble's ten Alexander-bodied Atlanteans were instantly recognisable due to their distinctive curved roofline. Even though there were so few of them they popped up in a variety of locations. On 15 April 1978 No. 1871 was photographed crossing Penwortham Bridge in Preston on a local service from Tardy Gate.

At one time Ambleside had three and Kendal had two of the batch for working the long 555 service. Kendal's No. 1875 has stopped opposite Windermere station on 20 April 1976 and is showing the destination of Kirkby Lonsdale, which is not actually on the route. Lancaster can just be seen underneath and it is likely that the blind has slipped. There was usually a healthy load of passengers waiting at this stop.

The PD3s lingered on Merseyside until 1981, after which the city services were mainly in the hands of Atlanteans. New in 1976, Park Royal-bodied No. 1398 is seen in St John's Lane in Liverpool city centre on 9 April 1983.

This spectacular sight depicts eight of Ribble's Atlanteans from a total of fifty double-deckers which were used on private hires to Heaton Park on the occasion of Pope John Paul II's visit to Manchester on 31 May 1982. They are Nos 1494/08/512/307/50/406/90/510. Olympians and Bristol VRTs were also used.

In 1974 Carlisle had an allocation of five short Leopards for use on its rural routes. They were predominantly used on services 631/3/41/3/4. No. 655 was residing in Carlisle bus station between duties on 8 August 1977.

Even though it had a much smaller allocation, Ambleside had six short Leopards amongst its ranks. These were again required to work routes that traversed typical country roads. Nos 651/50/62 were tucked away inside the garage on 20 April 1976 after a day's work. Opened in 1931, Ambleside garage was closed in 1989 when the Kendal and Ulverston operations passed to Stagecoach Cumberland.

Brand-new Leyland National No. 697 is seen parked alongside the paint shop at Frenchwood on 13 August 1976. This was one of a batch of twenty-nine 11.3-metre (37-foot) B49F Nationals numbered 687 to 715. It later received a white band.

No. 398 was one of the original two-door Nationals which had spent nearly a decade at Preston when it was pictured in Fylde Road on 9 May 1982. It is passing under the ever-shrinking WCML Railway Bridge, so called because the headroom diminished from 15 feet to 14 feet over a number of years without any physical changes being 'made'.

The dual-purpose Leopards were real workhorses and put in the miles on both local and medium-distance express routes over the years. Then allocated to Kendal and formerly of Blackpool and Liverpool garages, No. 921 is seen on 30 April 1980 in Kentsford Road climbing away from Kents Bank on a local journey from Cark to Grange-over-Sands.

On 9 May 1976 Lancaster's No. 828 was one of a number of buses employed on a private hire. It is seen parked outside Carnforth station whilst its passengers enjoyed a trip behind former LNWR 2-4-0 No. 790 *Hardwicke* to Grange-over-Sands and back. Billed as 'The North Western' and running as 1L00, *Hardwicke* made four round trips on the day.

Three of Ribble's garages had an allocation of ten or fewer vehicles. These were Bury (eight), Grange (eight) and Skipton (ten). In 1974 the ten buses allocated to Skipton consisted of short Leopards Nos 631/73, Leopard coaches Nos 796 and 832, dual-purpose Leopards Nos 765/67/72, 'white lady' Atlanteans Nos 1276/8 and lowbridge Atlantean No. 1668. The short Leopards were usually employed on local services based around Skipton whilst the DPs were often to be seen on the X27 to Liverpool and the 'white ladies' on the X43 to Manchester. *Above:* No. 1278, repainted into poppy red in 1973, is seen at the old Skipton bus station in 1974. *Below:* Leopard No. 631 is seen in an earlier view at the same location on a short working X43 (293) to Earby. Skipton garage was closed in 1976 with some buses retaining a presence at the West Yorkshire garage. Pennine Motors acquired the Ribble garage premises, which were still standing in 2023. (Malcolm Jones)

The jointly operated P4 service is featured a number of times in this book as for a number of years it was somewhat of a novelty to see Ribble buses working a local service. PD3/5s were just one of the types so employed and No. 1840 is seen approaching the terminus in Barry Avenue on 6 May 1977.

Six of the Burlingham-bodied PD3/4s found their way across the oceans to Hong Kong. Nos 1503/16 were actually used in service with China Motorbus whilst Nos 1533/59/76/82 acted as Driver Training buses. Now discarded, No. 1582 (T4) is seen amongst the scrap metal at Causeway Bay on 24 October 1981. The elevated road in the background leads to the cross-harbour tunnel.

More variety on the P4 and MCCW-bodied Atlantean No. 1690 is seen in Walker Street on 11 November 1976. The P4 had a peculiar routeing out of Preston. At one time in ran along Tenterfield Street and Lawson Street to join Walker Street until the construction of Ring Way severed this route in the late 1960s.

Short Leopard No. 663 had for a long time been associated with Penrith garage but was displaced in 1979. It had a short spell at Preston before being withdrawn and sold to the Isle of Man National Transport (as No. 5 and registered F459 MAN). It too is seen in Walker Street on the P4 on 27 September 1979. It was scrapped on the island in 1984.

Ambleside's short Leopard No. 660 was photographed on Rothay Bridge, crossing the River Rydal at Ambleside, on 21 April 1976 whilst returning from Dungeon Ghyll. This is a journey No. 660, along with its five compatriots, would have made countless times in the mid-1970s.

No. 660 was another of the ten 'Shorties' to cross the Irish Sea to the Isle of Man, as part of a second tranche of five in 1980. On 21 August 1982 and now numbered 1 in the IOMNT fleet, it was to be found in Parliament Square in the centre of Ramsey. This one returned to the mainland and was scrapped by Jones of Carlton in May 1984.

Dual-purpose Leopard No. 913 doesn't need a signpost to tell it which way to go. It is seen at Pullwood Bay on the B5286 between Hawkshead and Ambleside. (Ian Derrick)

Similar bus No. 900 is seen at the back of Preston bus station sometime in 1980 to a backdrop of demolition works as the old John Booth's 1871 foundry (originally known as the Phoenix Ironworks) is razed to the ground. (Ian Derrick)

Another representative of Ribble's ten Alexander-bodied Atlanteans was exiled in Carlisle for a number of years in the 1970s. No. 1873 is seen in Bank Street in the city centre on 8 August 1977. Service 669 was interworked with the 668 and ran from Belle Vue to Blackwell, with certain journeys extended to the Black Lion at Durdar.

With plenty of seats to spare, similar bus No. 1875 is seen in Blackhall Road in Kendal on 9 August 1977 whilst working a service 555 journey from Keswick to Lancaster. This bus was on home ground being one of two allocated to Kendal at the time, the other being No. 1876. The Nags Head is now known as Galloway House and is a listed building.

In 1965/6 Ribble broke with tradition and bought a batch of ten Plaxton-bodied Bedford VAMs, numbered 854–63. These had thirty-two seats and were fitted with a number of tables and were intended for use as touring coaches. They operated for four seasons and were disposed of in 1969. The former No. 858 is seen at Blackpool on 5 June 1982, then in the ownership of Davies Coaches of Chadderton.

Thirty Plaxton-bodied Leopards, Nos 946–75, joined the fleet in 1969 and gave around ten years of service. They were originally in Ribble's red and cream livery. Nos 954/9 were photographed in Askew's yard (dealer) in Barnsley on 10 September 1979. Both had been allocated to Aintree garage.

Penrith's Bristol RESL No. 314 is seen crossing the Settle to Carlisle railway line at Low House near Armathwaite whilst working a service 631 duty from Carlisle to Penrith via Cotehill and Kirkoswald. The signal box was constructed by the Midland Railway and opened in 1900. In 2023 the local services were operated by Fellrunner to very infrequent timetables – typically one journey on one day of the week. (Ian Derrick)

Both Aintree and Bootle had an allocation of single-door Bristol RESLs but whilst Bootle's were Marshall bodied, those at Aintree were ECWs. Two of the former, Nos 292/82, are seen at rest alongside the Liver Building in Water Street in Liverpool on 30 August 1976. They are unusual choices for the 57 and 58 services, which would normally be worked by double-deckers.

The decimation of Ribble's fleet began in 1986, firstly when the Carlisle and Penrith garages were transferred to Cumberland in February and subsequently by the formation of the North Western Roadcar Company in September when the Merseyside and Wigan garages were hived off. North Western adopted this rather attractive livery which is seen on Park Royal-bodied Atlantean No. 427, the former Ribble No. 1332, at Wythenshawe bus station on 19 August 1989.

Another former Ribble Park Royal-bodied Atlantean was No. 1380, which is seen in the colours of The Bee Line Buzz Company at Stockport bus station on 20 March 1993. Unlike No. 1332, this one looks rather scruffy. Bee Line had been formed in January 1987 with a fleet of minibuses. It was taken over by Ribble in September 1988 and then passed with Ribble to Stagecoach in April 1989, who then sold it on to the Drawlane Group in October when it became a subsidiary of North Western.

Plaxton-bodied Leopard No. 961 was one of six coaches allocated to Grange in the mid-1970s for use on day trips and private hire work. It is seen passing St Oswald's Church in the centre of Grasmere. The church dates from the fourteenth century and is a Grade I listed building. (Ian Derrick)

Service 514 had just one return journey on one day of the week. Leopard No. 475 had left Ulverston at 12.20 bound for Cunsey Road End from where it returned at 13.11. The driver has paused the bus at Newby Bridge on its return journey to enable the photographer to obtain this picture. The date is Thursday 11 August 1977.

Ribble disposed of more of its Park Royal-bodied Atlanteans towards the end of the 1980s. This was somewhat ironic as it later bought some similar buses from Southdown for its operations in Manchester. Hyndburn Transport acquired at least three and the former No. 1383 (Hyndburn No. 208) is seen in Accrington bus station on 9 March 1991.

By 1982 Burnley's allocation of Leopards had mainly been replaced by Nationals. However, two Bristol RESLs were to be found in the garage yard on 22 April: No. 347 with a white band and No. 360 without. Burnley garage was swept away in 2000 and the site is now occupied by a supermarket.

Fylde Borough Transport bought a trio of Ribble's 1965 Weymann-bodied dual-purpose Leopards through a dealer in February 1979. These had been Nos 808/10/6 in the fleet. The first two entered service with Fylde in May 1980 with the third following in October. No. 31 had been Ribble No. 810 and is seen (*above*) at Southport on 17 August 1980 having participated in the Ribble Enthusiast's Road Run from Blackpool to Southport. All three were withdrawn in 1982 and the former Ribble No. 808 (Fylde No. 30) passed to the *Blackpool Evening Gazette* for use as a promotional vehicle. It is seen (*below*) in Queen's Terrace in Fleetwood on the occasion of the first 'Tram Sunday' – 14 July 1985.

Service 685 from Carlisle to Newcastle was jointly operated with United Automobile and was scheduled to take three hours for the 55-mile journey. From 1973 Ribble standardised on the Duple-bodied Leopard for its coach requirements. No. 1108 was one of twenty-three obtained in 1978/9 and is seen laying over in Newcastle's Marlborough Crescent bus station on 4 April 1979 before making the journey back to Carlisle. The bus station was closed in 1983 and the site has been redeveloped.

Similar bus No. 1135 was new in 1980 and was on a private hire when photographed outside Preston's Guild Hall on 18 June 1983. Subsequent deliveries were branded as National Travel West until 1983, by which time the Tiger had superseded the Leopard. However the NTW coaches were integrated into the Ribble fleet in May 1984.

Ribble took delivery of ten ECW-bodied Bristol RELLs in 1968 fitted with Leyland engines. Another thirty soon followed, which had Gardner power units. Still sporting Ribble livery, No. 246 was one of a handful allocated to Preston to work the jointly operated P2 service. It is seen on Fishergate Railway Bridge on 27 June 1974 heading for Penwortham.

Eight of the type were allocated to Carlisle throughout most of the 1970s. No. 256 is seen in Carlisle bus station on 26 May 1976. They were generally employed on local city services 665 (Kingstown) and 670 (Wetheral Green). The last of the type were withdrawn from service in 1982.

Leopard No. 489 was caught on camera on the B5281 close to where it joins the A5092 at Gawthwaite, on 30 April 1980, with the 13.00 service 511 from Ulverston to Millom. This was one of three return journeys on Monday–Friday with there being just two on a Saturday.

Similar Leopard No. 480 is seen in Station Road at the Cark Engine Inn on the same day. This is a service 531 (not 530), which had left Kendal at 08.01 and would return to Grange on reaching Cartmel at 09.13. Nos 480/9 were both transferred to Fleetwood the following month.

Never having been prolific with all-over advert buses, a number of Olympians received them in the late 1980s. No. 2108 is seen setting out from Preston bus station for Wigan on American Independence Day, 4 July 1987. In 2023 the 125 was the principal service to Bolton.

Also seen on the 125 to Wigan, a few days later, is No. 2152. It was photographed in Lancaster Road in Preston and is advertising the centenary of the *Lancashire Evening Post*.

To illustrate the isolation of some of the Cumbria villages served by Ribble in the 1970s another view of Leopard No. 480 is included as it passes through the totally deserted village of Allithwaite on 30 April 1980. It is working the 15.33 service 533 from Kendal to Newby Bridge via Grange-over-Sands and Kents Bank. The author's long-time friend the late Roy Dickinson is looking on. (Ian Derrick)

One of Ribble's ten ECW-bodied dual-purpose Bristol RELHs, No. 1019, is seen in Hall Ings in the centre of Bradford on 10 December 1977. Service 281 was a remnant of the 'J' routes which were operated jointly with the 'Yorkshire Pool' operators. It ran from Leeds to Blackpool (and vice versa) via Bradford, Keighley, Skipton, Blackburn and Preston amongst other places. The original 281 had run between Colne and Skipton.

This is a view of the rear section of Leyland National No. 423, having incurred severe fire damage, awaiting a decision at Frenchwood on its fate. The location of the damage would suggest it has suffered an engine fire. (Ian Derrick)

Leopard No. 478 had been a Penrith bus for a number of years. However it didn't look like it would see much more service when it was photographed alongside the Frenchwood paint shop on 24 September 1977.

Burnley and Morecambe garages were used as the collection points for withdrawn buses. *Above:* Looking somewhat worse for wear are Atlanteans Nos 1684/69, which were awaiting their fate at Burnley on 3 August 1974. *Below:* Just a week later, at Morecambe, the photographer came across another group of withdrawn buses, all still in Ribble livery. They are MCCW-bodied Leyland PD3/5 No. 1774, Burlingham-bodied Leyland PD3/4 No. 1535 and MCCW-bodied Leyland PDR1/1 No. 1659; similar bus No. 1656 is partially visible on the extreme left. Next stop would be the breakers yard for these buses.

Besides the many breakers yards in the Barnsley area, a tradition which continues to this day, there were also a number of bus dealers, one of which was Paul Sykes. *Above:* On 22 January 1975 a number of former Ribble coaches were present in the yard. From the left they are Plaxton-bodied Leopards Nos 743/31/36/54 with ex-north Western Harrington-bodied Leopard No. 1062 (150) sandwiched in between. Nos 1656/69 are the lowbridge Atlanteans on the end of the line. *Below:* This impressive line-up of former Ribble Leopards was photographed in Sykes' Yard on 23 May 1978 and comprised Nos 554/52/60/48/53/84, 602, 569/67/79/19.

The end of the road for most buses would be the scrapyard where they would be systematically or brutally dismantled. *Above:* On 23 May 1978 Atlantean No. 1688 was in a sorry state in Paul Sykes' yard at Blacker Hill on the outskirts of Barnsley. Its final garage allocation had been Preston. *Below:* In an equally distressed state was MCCW-bodied Leyland PD3/5 No. 1798 when it was photographed in Ken Askin's yard on the same day. It doesn't look to be in any fit state to make the trip to Preston. The Titan had latterly been based at Ormskirk.

Although Ribble is now but a distant memory, its successor Stagecoach did celebrate what would have been the centenary year of the company in 2019. On 22 May 2022 Stagecoach ADL Enviro40D No. 10030 was taking part in a vintage bus running day organised by the Ribble Vehicle Preservation Trust (RVPT). It is seen on Morecambe Promenade wearing the pre-deregulation 1980s nationalised Ribble livery. Scania No. 15566 carried a version of the red Timesaver livery. Arriva and Transdev also commemorated Ribble's centenary.

In 2021 Stagecoach produced an even more impressive commemorative livery, which was applied to ADL Scania No. 15305. This was one of a batch of buses that were branded for use on the X2 between Preston and Liverpool. However throughout 2021 it was a regular choice for the Saturday/Sunday only single-journey X8, which ran from Chorley to Keswick and back in the summer months only. It is seen at Grasmere on a damp 11 September.